Series/Number 06-006

The Legitimacy of Opposition: The Change of Government in Ireland in 1932

FRANK MUNGER
University of North Carolina

 SAGE Publications/London/Beverly Hills

For information address:

SAGE PUBLICATIONS, Ltd.,
St. George's House/44 Hatton Garden
London EC1N 8ER

SAGE PUBLICATIONS, INC.
275 South Beverly Drive
Beverly Hills, California 90212

International Standard Book Number 0-8039-9909-7

Library of Congress Catalogue Card No. L.C. 74-84260

FIRST PRINTING

Copyright © 1975 by SAGE Publications, Ltd.

Printed by Wells & Blackwell Ltd., Loughborough, Leics.

LIST OF TABLES

The Legitimacy of Opposition:
The Change of Government in
Ireland in 1932

FRANK MUNGER

Little hint of the significance of the 1932 general election is provided by the standard histories and biographies. Brian Inglis (1965: 211) summarizes it in a sentence: "In 1932 he (De Valera) was able to win a majority at a General Election, and to take office." Denis Gwynn (1933:238-239) provides more detail, but is equally matter-of-fact:

> Long before the polling had taken place, Cosgrave knew that his party were doomed to defeat, in spite of all his efforts. When the results were known before the end of February, the extent of de Valera's progress was revealed. He had won a number of seats, at the expense of the Labour Party and the Independents as well as the Cosgrave Party; and with 72 seats, Fianna Fail was much the largest party in the new Dail. Cosgrave's followers had been reduced from 66 to 57, and the Labour Party had decreased from 10 to 7. Even its Parliamentary leader, Mr. T. J. O'Connell, had been thrown out, and his place had to be filled by a young railwayman, Mr. William Norton. Of the Independents, a few were new-comers, more likely to support de Valera than Cosgrave; but even with their assistance, the seven members of the Labour Party held the balance of power. That they would support Cosgrave after all the bitter attacks of Labour upon his Ministry in recent years was unthinkable. It was clear that de Valera had at last regained his position as the national leader: and at the first meeting of the Dail he was elected President in Cosgrave's place.

Donal O'Sullivan (1940: 285) emphasizes the events that followed the election:

AUTHOR'S NOTE: *The research for this paper was made possible by grants from Syracuse University and from the Rockefeller Foundation Program in Constitutional Democracy. I am appreciative also of the assistance and counsel provided me by Desmond Roche, Senior Research Adviser, Institute of Public Administration, Dublin; John Whyte, Lecturer in Politics, Queen's University, Belfast; and by the late George O'Brien, Professor of Economics, University College, Dublin. The above are not, of course, responsible in any way for my assertions and interpretations.*

When the Dail reassembled on March 9, 1932 Mr. Frank Fahy, a member of Fianna Fail, was elected Chairman of the House on a purely party vote and Mr. Michael Hayes, who had filled the post with distinction since 1922, became a private member. Mr. Fahy proved to be a capable and impartial Chairman, but the view was expressed that the occupancy of the Chair should not be determined by the varying changes of political fortune. Mr. De Valera was thereupon elected President of the Executive Council by 81 votes to 68, there being no other nomination for the office. The sitting was then suspended for a short time and, when it was resumed, the new President announced, in Irish, that his appointment had been approved by the Governor-General.

Sean O'Faolain (1939) concludes:

It was a strange event. Here, by sheer weight of persistence, by his own self-belief, by hammering day in and day out for ten years on the one idea of an independent Ireland, by refusing to admit a single error of judgement, or the slightest divagation from his ideal, De Valera was once more at the head of Irish affairs; but he was now at the head of the government of a state against which he had fought in arms, and against which he had protested passionately by every work. The people were at least sufficiently tolerant, and sufficiently satisfied with his earnest assertion of his own honesty, to yield him again their trust.

Strangely enough none of the four[1] refers to what must seem to an outside observer the strangest aspect of all. Ireland had won its national independence only ten years before. The national movement had at once dissolved in civil war. De Valera had come to head the Republican government and, after his party's defeat in arms by the forces of the Irish Free State, he had turned once again to political action. Within a decade he had succeeded in winning plurality support in a general election. Even more remarkably, the government that had defeated him in the field permitted him to triumph through the ballot. From our present acquaintance with political processes in new nations, we know how strange these events are. What seemed to the Irish natural, normal, even inevitable, has occurred in few other places. Within ten year's time Ireland had established out of civil war what has been described as a "rare" and "exotic" form of government, one acknowledging "the right to participate in governmental decisions by casting a vote, the right to be represented, and the right of an organized opposition to appeal for votes against the government in elections and in parliament," (Dahl, 1966: xi-xii). This paper represents an effort to explain how so great a change could so quickly take place.

The military phase of the Irish struggle for national independence ended with the truce of July 11, 1921. Negotiations were then opened for a general settlement. The resulting compromise – described by the British as "Articles of Agreement" and by the Irish as a Treaty – was attacked on three main grounds. First, the Treaty implicitly accepted the partition of the island of Ireland by permitting six counties of Ulster to secede upon the act of the Parliament of Northern Ireland. Secondly, the Treaty was clothed in the symbols of royalty and Empire; this conflict came to centre upon the inclusion of a prescribed oath of faithfulness to the King. Third, the Treaty authorized use by the British Navy of certain specified ports and other facilities in Ireland. Within these limits the proposed new government, to be styled the Irish Free State (Saorstat Eireann), would possess self-government and fiscal autonomy.

The Irish national movement embraced three principal organizations. As a political party it was termed Sinn Fein. Following the general election of 1918 the Sinn Fein members elected to the British House of Commons from Ireland met separately in Dublin, called themselves Dail Eireann, and proclaimed a Republic of Ireland with the Dail as its legislative assembly. The army of the Republic, widely known as the Irish Republican Army or IRA, was *de jure* subordinate to Dail Eireann. Eamon De Valera, as the president both of the Dail and of Sinn Fein, was frequently described as the President of the Republic of Ireland.

The Treaty was submitted for ratification to Dail Eireann. De Valera, who had not personally participated in the negotiations, submitted a counter-proposal, the so-called Document No. 2. While accepting the provisions for partition included in the Treaty, De Valera's draft differed in its use of the symbols of nationhood and in limiting the grant of the ports to a period of five years subject to renewal only by a new treaty freely negotiated. In essence it called for the recognition of a republic "externally associated" with the British Commonwealth of Nations.[2] The Treaty's supporters, led by Arthur Griffith and Michael Collins, insisted that the alternative terms would not be accepted by Great Britain and that rejection of the Treaty would mean resumption of the war. On January 7, 1922, the Treaty was ratified by a vote of 64 to 57.

With ratification the national movement divided. De Valera resigned the presidency of Dail Eireann and moved into opposition. Griffith was elected in his place. Unsuccessful efforts were made to use Sinn Fein, a majority of whose members opposed the Treaty, to bridge the gap. The army also divided; a majority of the volunteer rank-and-file supported its own group of anti-Treaty leaders, but the bulk of the headquarters staff and the Dublin Active Service Unit followed Collins into the Free State. By agreement two panels of Sinn Fein candidates, one for the Treaty and one against it, were nominated for the general election held June 16, 1922.

This election agreement or "pact" was intended to avoid open contests within Sinn Fein and called for the formation of a coalition government with a pro-Treaty majority after the election. However, additional candidates were nominated by the Labour party, the Farmers, and independents, and the election actually produced a pro-Treaty majority of 92 to 36. Fortified by this evidence of popular support and before the new Dail met, government forces attacked the headquarters of the anti-Treaty IRA group in the Four Courts in Dublin. Anti-Treaty political leaders, including De Valera, joined the anti-Treaty military leaders and the civil war had begun.

In January 1923 the deputy chief of staff of the Republican army, Liam Deasy, was captured by Free State forces. The following month Austin Stack, the second-ranking political leader after De Valera, was taken. In April Chief of Staff Liam Lynch was killed in the Knockmealdown Mountains. With Lynch gone De Valera assumed greater authority over the Republican forces and on April 30 he ordered the army to "suspend aggressive action". When the Free State forces continued to fight Frank Aiken, the new IRA chief of staff, on May 24, 1923, ordered the Republicans to "cease fire" and "dump arms". There was a significant difference between this and an order to surrender; arms were to be hidden for later use. By this time about 12,000 anti-Treaty soldiers and sympathizers were in prison. The war had not been without cost for the Free State government. Only a few weeks after the surrender of the garrison in the Four Courts Arthur Griffith, president of the executive council, had died of a stroke. Ten days later his successor, Michael Collins, was ambushed and killed on a back-country road in Cork, to be succeeded in turn by William T. Cosgrave. From September 1922, to July 30, 1923, civil war casualties totalled 665 killed and 3,000 wounded. Property damage, exclusive of the cost of prosecuting the war, came to £30 million.[3]

With peace returning the government called a general election for August 1923. Although De Valera was now "on the run" he announced his candidacy for his old constituency in Clare. As he had promised, he appeared to address an election meeting at Ennis on August 15 and, amid a flurry of gunfire, was arrested. He was elected while in prison — heading the poll — and the Republicans, using the Sinn Fein name, secured 44 seats to 63 for the government party in a house of 153. After his release from prison the following year De Valera, like the other Republican deputies, refused to take his seat in what was described as an "usurping legislature". By 1926, however, he had reconsidered this policy and proposed a new approach. The oath to the king, a contradiction to the prior oath taken to the Republic, was singled out as the central obstacle to national unity. De

Valera summoned an Ard Fheis or convention of Sinn Fein to act on a resolution declaring that if the oath were removed, entering the Free State parliament would be regarded "not as a question of principle but as a question of policy". The Sinn Fein party organization, still controlled by the most extreme members of the Republican movement, rejected this motion 223 to 218. Supported by most of the best-known (male) leaders of the party, De Valera resigned from Sinn Fein and established a new party, Fianna Fail, pledged to his policy.

The first general election to follow De Valera's creation of Fianna Fail came in June 1927. The result gave the new party 44 seats to 47 for Cumann na nGaedhal, the Irish name for the Cosgrave party, with the remaining seats scattered among smaller parties and independents. Before the Dail met again De Valera obtained an opinion from three legal authorities that deputies duly elected who refused to take the oath could not be deprived of their seats. The Fianna Fail deputies presented themselves but were refused admission. Cosgrave was re-elected president of the executive council. Then on July 10 Kevin O'Higgins, minister for external affairs, minister of justice, and vice-president of the executive council, was shot dead on a surburban Dublin street. The government reacted with a package of emergency legislation, one part of which would have required *candidates* for election to the Dail to take the oath. Passage of the bill would have forced Fianna Fail out of elective politics. Confronted with the prospect De Valera took the oath, describing it as an "empty formality", and led his followers into the Dail.

Fianna Fail, in combination with two minor parties, Labour and the National League, now possessed a majority of one vote in the Dail and was in a position to overturn the Cosgrave government. (The National League had been formed the previous year on the foundations of the old pre-war Irish Nationalist party under the leadership of Captain William Redmond, the son of one of its most prominent leaders.) De Valera agreed to supply the vote to place in office a coalition of Labour and the National League, pledged to open negotiations with Great Britain for an amendment to the Treaty that would eliminate the oath, but when the vote was taken one of the League deputies absented himself and the casting vote of the Speaker retained Cosgrave in power. Cosgrave promptly dissolved the Dail and a subsequent general election in September, 1927 increased the Cumann na nGaedhal representation to 62, less than a majority but sufficient to govern with the support of friendly independents and farmers' deputies. Fianna Fail consolidated its position as the opposition party with 57 seats and De Valera — within limits discussed below — accepted the role of leader of the opposition. The results of the elections from 1922 through 1932 are summarized in Table 1. [4]

TABLE 1. Party Representation in Dail Eireann, 1922-1932

	1922	1923	1927 (June)	1927 (Sept)	1932
Cumann na nGaedhal	58	63	47	62	57
Sinn Fein	35	44	5	–	–
Fianna Fail	–	–	44	57	72
Labour	17	14	22	13	7
Farmers	7	15	11	6	4
National League	–	–	8	2	–
Independents	11	17	16	13	13
Total	128	153	153	153	153

Sources: The table is adapted from McCracken (1958: 73). The pro-Treaty panel in 1922 has been classified with Cumann na nGaedhal and the anti-Treaty panel with Sinn Fein. A slightly different tabulation is given in Hogan (1945: 97) and still different results are recorded in O'Sullivan (1940: 62, 133, 193, 221, and 285). The discrepancies are produced by the problems of categorizing deputies of varying degrees of independence elected in a system of proportional representation based upon the single transferable vote.

Cosgrave's majority in the Dail elected in September, 1927 was a fragile one and when he lost a routine division, he resigned. Sean T. O'Kelly, De Valera's deputy, thereupon nominated De Valera but Labour and the other minor groups took fright at the emphasis on Republicanism and declined to support him. Cosgrave was then re-elected but his position remained weak as he approached the 1932 general election. With the international economic crisis exerting a depressing effect upon the Irish economy and with a high probability of De Valera's return to power public interest was high and a record proportion of the electorate voted.[5] (McCracken, 1958: 80)

	% of Electorate Voting
1922	62
1923	61
1927, June	68
1927, Sept.	69
1932	77

The election was orderly and without serious disturbance. As widely anticipated, Fianna Fail received the largest number of seats in the Dail, 72. The party actually obtained pluralities in 21 of the 29 constituencies, but was kept from a majority by the electoral system of proportional representation. Although Labour lost strength − and its leader, T. J. O'Connell, who was defeated in his own constituency − it emerged with the balance of power. De Valera's majority in the Dail would be dependent upon the anticipated support of the Labour party. (The Round Table, 1931-32: 493-497).

It is of the greatest importance but of much difficulty to determine precisely what happened next. That De Valera took office without serious incident is known. Two alternatives remain, however: first, that there was no serious hesitation on the part of major officials in the Cosgrave government about turning over power; second, that a substantial number of government officials seriously contemplated resisting the change but, either out of fear of the consequences, or through their inability to secure the agreement of other persons considered necessary to the plot, or out of whatever combination of unwanted circumstances, could not bring it off. The selection of the correct alternative determines what it is that is to be explained and, therefore, the kind of explanation that is appropriate.[6]

Writing thirty years and more later, Coogan (1966: 70) asserts: "On the Fianna Fail side, there were widespread rumours that elements in Cumann na nGaedhal would not allow them to take office. Accordingly, as the Fianna Fail deputies filed into the government benches, almost every man of them carried a revolver in his pocket." Setting aside the question of the exact proportions of the deputies who were armed, other evidence confirms the view that many Fianna Fail leaders considered resistance to the change of government a serious possibility. While providing testimony to the climate of suspicion within Ireland at the time that fact does not in itself, of course, confirm that such resistance was actually contemplated. The fears of the party leaders were, however, reflected in specific charges. On February 26 the Fianna Fail party newspaper, *The Irish Press,* reported as news a rumour that two members of the Cosgrave Cabinet were plotting with army pensioners to arrange a *coup d'état,* a report immediately repudiated by Cosgrave as "grotesquely untrue" (The Round Table, 1931-32: 493-497).

The most detailed exposition of this alleged plot is found in the only biography of De Valera to assert that such an event occurred. MacManus (1962: 281-282) writes:

When in March 1932 De Valera's party took over the reins of government there were underground rumblings of which the public were completely unaware at the time and of which even today there is no general knowledge. After the Civil War Free State Ministers had declared that they would drive "that man" out of political life for ever, and there was still a group in existence who were determined to

> attempt it, by fair means or foul. Preparations were made as soon as the results of the General Election were announced for a *coup d'état* with the object of suppressing parliamentary government and of setting up a military dictatorship. De Valera was to be got rid of at any price. The conspirators included two former members of the Cosgrave Ministry and a group of Army and Police officers. The *putsch* was to be carried out by means of a secret army organisation.
>
> It was a desperate plot, and one which if put into operation, could not have failed to plunge the country once more into civil war. But it miscarried. Mr. Cosgrave refused to have anything to do with it, and a high ecclesiastical dignitary to whom a rumour of what was on foot had come, let it be known that the Church would give it no countenance whatever. As a result the conspiracy was called off and the change of government was effected under conditions of peace.[7]

No specific source is cited for this statement. An author's foreword indicates that the work has been written "from the standpoint of an admirer" of De Valera, but "I have neither sought nor received any assistance from the subject of this biography. He was not even aware that it was being written"(MacManus, 1962: 6, 7).[8] The author of this paper has encountered only three specific allegations that might be used to document MacManus's indictment. Shortly after the change of government De Valera charged in a debate in the Dail that General Richard Mulcahy had engaged in conversations with British officials preparatory to a possible *coup d'état.* Mulcahy denied the accusation. A few days later De Valera withdrew it. A second version of the story named Ernest Blythe, vice-president of the executive council in the Cosgrave government, and General Michael Brennan, the army chief of staff, as the individuals involved.[9] Blythe and Brennan were close friends — they had shared a cell while imprisoned by the British — but the charge seems amply refuted by the fact that Brennan was permitted to serve out his term as chief of staff by the De Valera government and was then twice reappointed.

As this suggests, the strongest evidence against the existence of such a conspiracy lies in the subsequent behaviour of Fianna Fail governments. De Valera remained in power for 16 years after 1932. With the full authority of the state behind them his party had ample opportunity to investigate the charges and every incentive to make public any damaging evidence found. But there is no pattern of dismissals to suggest the elimination of plotters from government office[10] nor was any effort made by Fianna Fail to perpetuate such charges in later political campaigns — despite the fact that the ultimate responsibility for the civil war remains a staple of Irish political debate down to the present day.

The most difficult accusation to evaluate is, however, the third suggestion: that General Eoin O'Duffy, chief of the Garda Siochana, the national police force, was involved in a plot to prevent the change of government. (Since the Garda is an unarmed force, such a conspiracy would presumably have involved some among General O'Duffy's former associates in the army.) O'Duffy was retained in office by the De Valera government until 1934, when he was dismissed, but such a retention could be explained, of course, as politic while Fianna Fail felt its way into full power. Upon his death O'Duffy was given a state funeral by a later De Valera government, but that too could be explained away. On the other hand, it is not necessary to imagine that O'Duffy was involved in a conspiracy in 1932 to explain his dismissal and it is hard to think of a reason why the government would have kept public silence on the matter if they could have produced substantial evidence of an O'Duffy plot. Such evidence would have been particularly damaging after O'Duffy had been hailed as leader by the combined opposition to De Valera and had become the commander of the semi-fascist Blueshirt movement.[11]

Any conclusion must be partly speculative, but it is hardly surprising that the evidence should be less complete than might be wished. An attempt to determine what actually happened in 1932 within the Cosgrave government in its last days involves both an effort to demonstrate a negative and a judgement on a matter highly charged with political consequence, literally involving conviction for treason against the state. Between the two alternatives suggested above, however, the evidence points convincingly in the direction of the first: that there was no serious hesitation on the part of major officials in the Cosgrave government about turning over power. If any officials contemplated resistance they were few in number and unsuccessful in winning allies. The remainder of this paper, therefore, will be concerned with the effort to explain this (near) unanimous acceptance of the principle of party alternation in government.

At the first level of explanation this consensus concerning the legitimacy of opposition might be attributed to general characteristics of the society conducive to the acceptance of democratic processes. It has often been argued that economic development produces a social structure facilitative of democracy in political life. Seymour Lipset (1963), for example, has sought to demonstrate that stable democracies in Europe and the English-speaking world tend to be differentiated from dictatorships and unstable democracies by their per capita wealth, degree of industrialization and urbanization and level of education. Since Lipset includes Ireland in the category of stable democracies[12] it is possible to use his groupings to examine the applicability of this generalization to Ireland.

As indicators of economic and social development Lipset employs per capita income, number of persons per motor vehicle, thousands of persons per physician, number of radios per thousand persons, number of telephones, number of newspaper copies, percentage of employed males engaged in agriculture, per capita energy consumed, percentage of population in cities of over 20,000, percentage of population in cities of over 100,000, percentage of population in standard metropolitan areas, percentage literate, primary education enrolment per 1,000 persons, enrolment in post-primary education, and enrolment in higher education. He notes: "Not all the countries in each category were used for each calculation, as uniform data were not available for them all. For instance, the data available on Albania and East Germany are very sparse. The USSR was left out because a large part of it is in Asia."

TABLE 2. Indicators of Social and Economic Development

	Rank of Ireland Among 13 Stable Democracies	Higher Ranks Among 17 Unstable Democracies and Dictatorships
Per capita gross national product	13	6
Inhabitants per physician	12	10
% of labour force employed outside agriculture	13	6
% of pop. living in cities over 20,000	9	6
Daily newspaper circulation per 1,000	13	5
Radios per 1,000 pop.	13	10
% of pop. 5-19 in primary and secondary schools	6	1
Students in higher education per 1,000 pop.	11	9

Sources: Data are derived from Russett et al. (1964: 155-157, 202-206, 175-179, 49-53, 107-110, 118-122, 217-220, and 213-216) where further details can be found of the base periods used for comparison. One index has been reversed, that concerning employment in agriculture, to make the ranking commensurate with the others.

More complete data are now available through the *World Handbook of Political and Social Indicators,* but for a somewhat different collection of indices. In Table 2 Ireland is compared both with the group of stable democracies and the group of unstable democracies and dictatorships on eight indices derived from this source. On four of the eight Ireland stands at the bottom of the list among the 13 stable democracies; this includes what some might consider the most important index of all, per capita gross national product. On only one indicator is Ireland found in the top half of the distribution of stable democracies: primary and secondary school enrolments. Only on this measure is Ireland clearly above the group of nations classified as unstable democracies and dictatorships. On three of the eight indices Ireland would actually be placed in the bottom half of the distribution if ranked with the latter group.

The atypically high ranking for primary and secondary education is an interesting one, and may suggest a possible approach for further investigation of the relationships between social characteristics and political democracy. Obviously it is not independent of the political process and reflects a decision made through the political system to allocate fiscal resources to education. In terms of the other indicators of wealth, industrialization, and urbanization, which are more likely to be independent of political decisions, Ireland ranks low and below many nations less successful in maintaining democratic institutions. It is apparent that Ireland's acceptance of political opposition and party alternation in government cannot be explained in terms of such generalizations. From the perspective of the generalization that political development accompanies economic development Ireland stands as a deviant case, providing an opportunity to test the limits of the generalization and to explore other relevant variables. In attempting to explain the events of 1932, however, the generalization provides little guidance, suggesting only that Ireland's successful accomplishment of a change of government was doubly remarkable. An explanation of that event must be sought elsewhere.

A statement by Fianna Fail, published over the name of Eamon De Valera in the *Irish Independent* of February 11, 1932, asserted that the party sought a mandate:

1. To remove the Article of the Constitution which makes the signing of the Oath of Allegiance obligatory on members entering the Dail . . .

2. To retain the Land Annuities in the State Treasury . . . With two of the three million pounds involved the farmers can be relieved completely of the rates on their holdings. Another million is available for the relief of taxation, or for such purposes as the Dail may determine.

3. To submit to Counsel for their opinion the question of the obligation to make the other annual payments to Britain, including the pensions of the former R.I.C. and to act on the opinion obtained . . .

4. To organize systematically the establishment of the industries required to meet the needs of the community in manufactured goods . . . Suitable fiscal laws would be passed to give the protection necessary against unfair foreign competition.

5. To preserve the home market for our farmers and to encourage the production by them of our food requirements to the greatest extent possible.

6. To negotiate trade agreements that would secure for our

products preferences in foreign markets ... Machinery and other capital equipment for our industries will have to be purchased from abroad. We can in these purchases accord a preference to Britain in return for a preference in her markets for our agricultural produce.

7. To take the necessary powers to eliminate waste and extravagance in public administration ...

8. To endeavour by systematic effort to preserve the Irish language and make it again the spoken language of the people.

We pledge ourselves that, if elected in a majority, we shall not in the field of international relations exceed the mandate here asked for without again consulting the people.

We may add that we have no leaning towards Communism and no belief in Communistic doctrines ... We ask the electors not to allow themselves to be deceived by the misrepresentations of our opponents, and we pledge ourselves not to abuse their confidence (Moss, 1933: 206-209).

This was not a revolutionary programme, although there were revolutionaries abroad in the Ireland of that time. The IRA continued to function as an underground army still preparing to strike one day against the Free State for the Republic. As early as November, 1925, before De Valera's withdrawal from Sinn Fein to create Fianna Fail, an IRA convention had withdrawn allegiance from the "Government" headed by De Valera and had designated the Army Council as its highest authority. The IRA retained links with the political organizations of the Republicans for some time and made efforts to heal the split in Sinn Fein. By the time of the first 1927 general election, however, they apparently had severed all their ties to both Sinn Fein and Fianna Fail.[13] The IRA was itself pulling apart as some members sought to broaden its programme to include economic as well as national goals. Beginning in Donegal in 1924 Peadar O'Donnell (1963) an IRA leader, had launched a campaign urging farmers to withhold the so-called land annuities, payments on the bonds given to former landlords under some of the land purchase acts. O'Donnell was unable to secure official IRA sanction for this movement but in 1929 he joined with other left-wing IRA members to form Saor Eire, an organization whose avowed aim was the creation of "an independent revolutionary leadership for the working class and working farmers" to accomplish "the overthrow in Ireland of British imperialism and its ally, Irish Capitalism". Saor Eire was suppressed as communistic under the Public Safety Act of 1931, but was replaced in 1933 by the Republican Congress, with many of the same leaders. The IRA itself rejected the attempt to develop a radical economic programme and the members of the Congress were expelled.[14] In a separate series of developments on different premises James Larkin, earlier an active leader in the Communist

International had been elected to Dail Eireann in September 1927 as an independent candidate from North Dublin. Larkin was identified in newspaper accounts as a communist and made no effort to disavow the label. Although Larkin did not take his seat — he was refused admission to the Dail as an undischarged bankrupt, a condition resulting from an intra-union dispute — his Irish Workers League continued to function as a Marxist political party, (See Emmet Larkin, 1965).

De Valera was personally friendly with Larkin and had co-operated with him at the time of the crisis over the passage of the Public Safety Bill in 1927, but shared few of his more radical ideas. From Peadar O'Donnell's programme Fianna Fail borrowed a concern for the land annuities, but in a quite different form than the refusal to pay that O'Donnell urged upon the farmers. Since the payments were actually collected by the Irish government and transmitted to the British government for payment to the individual bondholders, Fianna Fail proposed that the annuities be collected in Ireland, but deposited in the Irish treasury for general use, including assistance to the farm population, leaving to the British the task of finding the money to pay off the bonds. In De Valera's eyes this did not constitute expropriation for two reasons: first, the Irish were being compelled to buy back lands that had originally been stolen from them in the British conquest of the island; second, in the financial settlement with Northern Ireland the British government had assumed responsibility for similar debts in the six counties.

The other major items in the Fianna Fail programme were the repeal of the oath and a protective tariff policy. If the repeal of the oath had been considered to imply a repudiation of the connection with the British Commonwealth it would have constituted a drastic step, but De Valera was careful to emphasize the limited character of the mandate he sought. To the discomfiture of his opponents, he subsequently justified the repeal of the oath on the grounds that the Statute of Westminster — in which they had taken great pride — had provided the authority. The repeal of the oath plus the withholding of the land annuities plus the protective tariff policy were in practice ultimately to involve the Free State in an economic war with Great Britain that was ruinous to the larger commercial farmers in the export trade, but this still lay in the future in 1932. For the moment the emphasis upon the substitution of tillage agriculture for the export of livestock was a promise of more employment for agricultural labourers. De Valera was also to pursue a more vigorous social policy than the mandate sought suggested, substantially increasing expenditures for housing and social welfare, but this too was far from clear when he was elected (Gwynn, 1933: 240-286).[15]

The relative conservatism of the Fianna Fail programme was explained both by political and personal considerations. The electoral strength of the radical left in Ireland had been sapped by steady emigration during the 1920s. Depressed economic conditions, particularly in the West where the radicals were strongest, had driven ambitious young people out of the country. Job preference in public and in some private employment was given to veterans of the National Army. Veterans of the Republican Army or known sympathizers found themselves harassed by the police (but see Briscoe, 1959: 211-216).[16] Successive Public Safety acts permitted imprisonment without trial other than by a military tribunal. All these pressures combined to encourage young Republicans to leave the country with a consequent weakening of the extreme left. It is at least plausible that the buildup of revolutionary strength in the early 1930s was produced by the closing off of opportunities for emigration by the world economic crisis, just as recruitment for both the British Army and the IRA had been encouraged during World War I by the forced suspension of emigration.

The personal consideration was De Valera's own conservatism. Although a zealot in the pursuit of national goals, he was not a radical and had no taste for radicalism. Although – like other Republicans – at one time under the ban of the Catholic Church, he was not anti-clerical in any conventional European sense. For those who believed that he meant what he said, this was one of the reassuring elements in the change of government. Of course, not everyone possessed that confidence. The report in the *Round Table* of the election campaign, for example, had assured its readers: "The man in the street is perfectly well aware that if Mr. De Valera obtains a majority in the Dail, his Government will not be in power for two months before the hedgerow heroes – who have diplomatically disappeared since the Military Tribunal was set up – assert their authority by their usual methods of the threat and the gun, and Mr. De Valera, as he has always done, will toe the line and do what he is told – if indeed he is not unceremoniously kicked out – and people of his Kerensky-like temperament usually are" (The Round Table, 1931-1932: 374-375). Some credence for such views was provided by local Fianna Fail party speakers who had talked of firing unpopular judges and abolishing the Criminal Investigation Division of the Garda. Undoubtedly, many IRA men worked for De Valera's election although others abstained from a political contest which they considered irrelevant.

For those who did believe De Valera, however, the programme he advanced was a guarantee that he would not seek to disturb either of the major institutional forces in Irish life outside its government, the Catholic Church and the capitalist economic structure. A protective tariff policy would produce some economic dislocation, but there would be advantaged as well as disadvantaged firms. The position of the Church in education and elsewhere would remain unimpaired. For those more dubious of De Valera's good intentions reliance could be placed upon the restraining influences of (1) his need for Labour support in the Dail; (2) the civil service; and (3) the army, all of which would hold him within the broad outlines of his mandate. In sum any threat generated by the change of government was perceived in terms of its hostile impact upon these individuals contained within the world of government rather than its impact upon the society as a whole. This is not to belittle it, of course; most instances of *coups d'état* have required nothing more. It does serve, however, to define the arena within which the threat was felt. The affected personnel will be considered under three headings: the politicians, the administrators, and the army.

In Ireland the most commonly presented explanation for the peaceful change of government in 1932 is a personal one; the credit is usually given to William T. Cosgrave. This was the interpretation widely presented in the appreciations prepared at the time of Cosgrave's death in 1965. De Valera has himself expressed a not dissimilar view. The full argument goes something like this. Cosgrave consistently pursued a policy of bringing the opposition into parliamentary life even though he realized it would inevitably mean his own defeat some day. Both Cosgrave and Blythe, his vice-president, insisted that changes of government would be necessary to complete the political education of the country. The entry of Fianna Fail into the Dail was forced by legislation that Cosgrave's government introduced. At that time Cosgrave prophesied that the legislation would in the long run prove more advantageous to the opposition than to the government. The acceptance of the oath by De Valera was eased by the loose way in which it was administered by the clerk. Although Cosgrave's personal responsibility for the clerk's action is unclear, he could certainly have prevented it and made the oath more objectionable to Fianna Fail. In 1932 Cosgrave headed the government which gave up office without incident.

All this is true, but only a part of the truth. Actually a similar argument can be made for De Valera. In his original letter to the press announcing that the Cabinet had split over the Treaty De Valera wrote: "There is a definite constitutional way of resolving our political differences — let us not depart from it . . ." In an effort to keep the decision within parliamentary channels he negotiated a pact with Collins that would have placed his followers in a minority position in the Dail and called for his own service in a coalition Cabinet in a subordinate capacity. When the civil war ended and the general election of 1923 was called De Valera sought to return the conflict to a political level by again offering himself as a candidate, promising that, if nominated, he would appear in public at

Ennis and "nothing but a bullet" would stop him. In his effort to find a political rather than a violent solution for the division of the country he broke Sinn Fein and created Fianna Fail. He then sought to make use of the constitutional provisions for the initiative to initiate action to repeal the oath from the constitution.

The only difficulty with the two arguments is that they leave an unanswered question: with both sides so committed to a political resolution of the conflict, how did a civil war ever happen to take place? The answer is that both De Valera and his opponents wanted to make the decision a political one, but each wanted the political decision to be made on his own terms. Until the pact had been negotiated and implemented De Valera was unwilling to condemn the military adventurism of the anti-Treaty elements in the army. (Whether his condemnation would have affected their behaviour in any way is another question.) The government in turn was unwilling to attempt to use the coalition government provided in the pact to resolve the military crisis in the Four Courts. (The coalition may have been made impossible in any case by the refusal of the British government to accept the kind of constitution that would have been required to make the pact workable.) When De Valera appeared at Ennis, he was arrested; the Publicity Department of the Free State government issued a statement: "He now tries to shelter himself behind the political campaign, but he must take his place with his associates and dupes . . .' After De Valera founded Fianna Fail and implied his willingness to accept the responsibility of parliamentary opposition if the oath were removed, the Cosgrave government blocked every effort made to meet his condition. Despite the fact that the Treaty had already been once amended by negotiation[17] Cosgrave declined even to raise the question of the oath with British representatives. When in April 1927 Dan Breen introduced a bill into the Dail to amend the constitution by repealing the oath, the government took the unusual step of refusing to allow the formality of a first reading. And when Fianna Fail, taking advantage of provisions in the existing constitution, proposed to force a referendum on the oath, Cosgrave pressed through a constitutional amendment eliminating the initiative procedure. All this is before making the obvious point, that for five years De Valera refused to enter the Dail because of an oath he eventually decided was an "empty formality". Each of the parties was fearful of making a concessión that would appear to compromise earlier taken positions. If Cosgrave secured a modification of the oath it might appear to imply that De Valera had been right all the time: harder bargaining over the Treaty could have secured greater concessions from the British. Until that admission was made, De Valera refused to play the parliamentary game; to accept the oath would be to deny his original stand that the terms of the Treaty were morally repugnant to an Irish Republican.

Between the two men it was De Valera who gave way in 1927. Denis Gwynn (1928: 142) comments: "Mr. Cosgrave was a shrewder judge of realities than the Opposition; and he believed that by drastic measures he could force even Mr. De Valera to swallow all the professions that he had renewed even a few months before. Events justified his belief; and instead of reverting to lawless methods, Mr. De Valera and his party bowed to a will stronger than his own . . ." It is only a partial view, however, that sees the outcome as a test of strength between the two men. From De Valera's view it was quite different. By amending the constitution to eliminate the initiative and referendum, the government had made Dail Eireann the only source of law. By prohibiting those opposed to the oath from offering themselves even as candidates to the Dail, the government had closed off every avenue of non-violent protest. To refuse now to take the oath would mean to redirect the Republican movement in a revolutionary direction. It would also undoubtedly mean De Valera's elimination from any major leadership role. His appeal was as the spokesman for a policy of political Republicanism. The civil war had already demonstrated that in an armed conflict he would be reduced to a Republican figurehead or less. The 1925 IRA convention had confirmed that impression by repudiating his leadership. Cosgrave had succeeded in maneuvring De Valera into a position in which all other alternatives were foreclosed but the oath or political extinction. Whether out of concern for the fate of Ireland if the main body of Republicans turned back toward violence, or out of concern for his own position of leadership, or — most probably — out of much concern of the one kind and a little of the other, De Valera took the oath. Cosgrave had won his gamble, but a gamble with high stakes, for the injury to Ireland might have been very great if the convinced Republicans had been driven out of politics and into the IRA. (When De Valera had gambled similarly in 1922, he had not been so fortunate in the outcome.)

In this sense the transition of 1932 had been predetermined in 1927 when De Valera agreed to play the game according to the government's rules. Both parties had anticipated that the side that first yielded would suffer thereby with the electorate and Cosgrave and his lieutenants expected that the second election of 1927 would bring substantial losses to Fianna Fail. The exact opposite proved to be the case. Although Cumann na nGaedhal gained ground in the autumn election, so did Fianna Fail. Rather than rebuke De Valera for his retreat from principle, the voters rewarded him for his responsibility. What 1927 began, 1932 confirmed.

In the interim period De Valera served as leader of the opposition in the

Dail. He did not observe all the niceties of the position. When the Dail reassembled Fianna Fail refused to second the nomination of the incumbent chairman, ignoring the precedent set by the Labour Party opposition. De Valera refused to serve as chairman of the Public Accounts Committee, an appointment set aside for the opposition leader. Partly successful efforts were made to discourage social contacts between Fianna Fail deputies and members of the government party. De Valera did, however, display surprising flexibility in parliamentary tactics. He inflicted his first defeat on the government a few weeks after the session began, by supplying the votes necessary to carry a motion offered by Captain Redmond criticizing the government's failure to do more for Irish veterans of the British army; it seemed an unlikely issue for his party to espouse, although it did possess the consistency of an implication that Great Britain had dishonoured its promises to its servicemen. Ministerial responsibilities were assigned in a "shadow Cabinet" and regular criticism of government policies conducted.

Fianna Fail continued, however, to disavow any acceptance of the political *status quo* as implicit in the position of parliamentary opposition. In a speech in the Dail in 1928 Sean Lemass declared:

> Fianna Fail is a slightly constitutional party. We are perhaps open to the definition of a constitutional party, but before anything we are a Republican party. We have adopted the method of political agitation to achieve our end because we believe, in the present circumstances, that method is the best in the interests of the nation and of the Republican movement, and for no other reason. Five years ago the methods we adopted were not the methods we have adopted now. Five years ago we were on the defensive, and perhaps in time we may recoup our strength sufficiently to go on the offensive. Our object is to establish a Republican Government in Ireland. If that can be done by the present methods we have, we will be very pleased, but, if not, we would not confine ourselves to them (Dail Eireann, Parliamentary Debates 22: 1615).

The following year De Valera expressed the view:

> I still hold that our right to be regarded as the legitimate Government of this country is faulty. You have secured a *de facto* position. Very well. There must be some body in charge to keep order in the community, and by virtue of your *de facto* position you are the only people who are in a position to do it. But as to whether you have come by that position legitimately or not, I say you have not come by that position legitimately. You brought off a *coup d'état* in the summer of 1922 (Dail Eireann, Parliamentary Debates 28: 1398).

Such provocative statements became less frequent through the passing years, necessarily so, for debates on who was responsible for the civil war gave way to debates on specific legislation proposed and needed.

This provides, of course, only an indication of the strategies pursued by the contending parties, not of the reasons why they genuinely, rather than tactically, accepted a political policy. What were the constraints, both external and internal, that held both parties within the confines of the parliamentary game? This is the point at which an accurate reading of the factual situation in 1932 becomes so important. If Cosgrave and others carried a policy of the acceptance of the change of government over the opposition of a second group disposed to resist, it would be necessary to look to: (1) what was distinctive in the outlook of each party; (2) the mechanisms of influence through which Cosgrave and his supporters imposed their will. If, on the other hand, the acceptance was unanimous or nearly so, it must be explained in other terms.

In the latter case the convenient handle used to describe such a consensus on the proper policy to be pursued is political culture: a set of attitudes, widely held by individuals in the society and conducive to certain kinds of behaviour. This is the alternative the interpretation made above leads toward. The convictions about legitimate behaviour generally felt by the Irish people and their political leaders called for respecting the verdict of an election and admitting to the role of government the victors in the electoral contest.

Only tentative suggestions can be made as to why this should have been true and − in a circular argument − the principal evidence that such a culture existed lies in the fact that it purports to explain.[18] It is possible, however, to speculate on the ingredients that may have produced such a political culture. The first might be Ireland's long tradition of parliamentary action. Setting aside the early experience with an Irish parliament that met in Dublin in the 18th century, Ireland was represented at Westminster in the British House of Commons pursuant to the provisions of the Act of Union from 1801 to 1922. The accomplishment of Catholic emancipation in 1829 permitted the native Irish to participate freely in parliamentary affairs, and the extension of the franchise plus the introduction of the secret ballot in the latter 19th century gave nationalists of one stamp or another majorities in most Irish constituencies. In their major goal of a separate status − Repeal of the Union in the earlier 19th century and what was later called Home Rule − the parliamentary representatives of Irish nationalism were never successful but they did succeed in securing many lesser advantages including the disestablishment of the Church of Ireland and a comprehensive land reform. A second consideration was coupled with the first: since 1898, when the grand jury system was abolished, Ireland has possessed elective local self-government with a broad franchise. Indeed one of the major elements of Sinn Fein strength during the struggle for independence was its control of county councils and, though no leader on either side of the Dail had served in the House of Commons[19] both Cosgrave and Sean T. O'Kelly, De Valera's deputy, had local government experience.

Third, the Irish were fortunate in the fact that the computation of party majorities was made through one of the few Free State institutions whose symbolic role predated the Treaty and the civil war split. The Dail had been the instrument through which the Republic of Ireland was reproclaimed — it had first been proclaimed by the Provisional Government at the time of the Easter Rising in 1916 — and the Republican oath taken by members of the Dail, of the IRA, and of the Irish Republican Brotherhood, read: ". . . I will support and defend the Irish Republic and the Government of the Irish Republic which is Dail Eireann . . ." This argument can be overstated. The legitimacy of the succession of Dails was disputed by the Republican side and the last Dail to receive unequivocal acceptance by both sides was the second Dail, suspended, never to meet again, by the attack on the Four Courts. The first Dail to meet after the 1922 election called itself the Third Dail to emphasize continuity, but the Republicans insisted it was illegitimate and the minority members of the second Dail continued to meet, calling themselves the Republic of Ireland. (For the more practical-minded, the fiction was not unrelated to an American legal dispute over the custody of revenues from the sale of Republican bonds.)[20] This "second Dail" continued to meet until 1938 when it delegated "the authority reposed in us to the army council" of the IRA, but its vitality had been sapped first by De Valera's withdrawal and then by Fianna Fail's entry into and participation in the other Dail Eireann.

A fourth ingredient of Irish political culture must also be identified, the close association of the Catholic Church with parliamentary institutions. The great achievement of Danial O'Connell a century before the Free State came into existence had been to bring the Church into politics. O'Connell's Catholic Association and his subsequent Repeal Association were carried into the individual parishes by the support of the parish priest. Two generations later Parnell was almost as dependent upon the priests for political organization and was broken when the hierarchy turned upon him. The Church had consistently supported those who espoused parliamentarianism and had condemned the advocates of physical force, the Fenians, the Irish Republican Brotherhood, and, after the Treaty, the Republicans. The significance of the Church's position was twofold. First, it has great influence upon the attitudes of the Irish people. The parallel with Spain is often brought forward, but is misleading in its implications. The Catholic Church in Ireland is influential not through its wealth or its influential connections with a military, landowning class, but through the intense devotion to Catholicism of the great mass of the population, both male and female. It is powerful, therefore, precisely through its ability to shape popular attitudes. Secondly, those political leaders who have been most resistant to clerical influence, the inheritors of the Republican tradition who defied their condemnation by the hierarchy after the Treaty, were not those who needed restraint in 1932 for they were the victors. The Church's influence was greatest upon the Cosgravites and its influence moved in the direction of respect for constitutional processes (a direction of movement eased by the absence of any revengeful anti-clerical tones in Fianna Fail oratory).[21]

A fifth possibility also exists, that the Irish were strongly influenced by a desire to imitate British governmental models and in particular to repudiate the frequent suggestions of British politicians and political journalists that the Irish were incapable of self-government. The suggestion cannot stand by itself. There were examples available for imitation other than Great Britain; only a year or two after the 1932 change of government, the Cosgrave/O'Duffy opposition to De Valera was talking much of Mussolini and the Corporate State. And there have been too many ex-British colonies that have rejected parliamentary forms to assume that the process is an automatic one. It is reasonable to suppose, however, that the Irish — located only a few miles across the Irish Channel from Great Britain and deeply embedded in the Western tradition — might have been more influenced by the desire to imitate and surpass.

Finally, some comment should be made on the point that both of the contending parties in 1932 were, in their origins, wings of the same national movement. Both De Valera and Cosgrave fought in the Easter Rising; both had been sentenced to death; both had been imprisoned. And so on. It would be unwise to give too much weight to that fact; there is much subsequent evidence that men who have been in prison together can jail one another when they are out. Yet it is obviously relevant and its relevance can be suggested by imagining the opposite possibility, that one of the parties in 1932 had been a Sinn Fein party of the Republican tradition and the other a Unionist party with a past record of opposition to Irish nationalism. Northern Ireland comes inevitably to mind. It is difficult to believe that the transition could have been so smooth.

This discussion of political culture is not, of course, unrelated to consideration of the impact of the change of government upon the administration and the army. The British tradition of deference to political majorities was probably most deeply implanted in the administrative class, which had been inherited almost intact from the days of Dublin Castle rule by the British Government in Ireland. This was one of the most remarkable of all aspects of the situation. Under the terms of the Treaty civil servants in Ireland were permitted to transfer to service in Northern Ireland or Great Britain. Those who did not request otherwise were automatically transferred into the Free State civil service under guarantees concerning their future tenure and conditions of employment established in the Treaty. Most elected to remain in Ireland because most were Irish. Since 1871 open competitive examination had been the normal method of recruitment and many Irish had seen government employment as highly attractive. Precise figures are unavailable for the service as a whole, but as of 1914 38 of the 48 highest ranking officials in Ireland were Irish in origin. These were divided almost equally between Catholic and Protestants. The proportions of native Irish and of Catholics undoubtedly were higher in the lower ranks (McDowell, 1964).[22]

Sentiment was occasionally expressed in favour of wholesale dismissals, but the costs would have been prohibitive. When at the 1924 Cumann na nGaedhal convention a resolution was offered: "That in our opinion the time has arrived when the late officials of the British Government . . . be dispensed with," Blythe, the Finance Minister, pointed out that under the terms of the Treaty it would have been necessary to add 17 years to the pension service of these men if they were dismissed. The resolution was withdrawn. There were not in any case suitable substitute experts nor did the civil service constitute an alien class that compelled replacement. Some effort was made to weed out Republicans. A declaration of allegiance to the Free State Constitution was made obligatory in both the national and local government services and local authorities were required to give priority in employment to demobilized soldiers of the Free State Army.

It was this civil service — plus ten years — that De Valera inherited. For administrators who had passed from the British service to the Free State the transition from Cosgrave to De Valera was no more abrupt.

TABLE 3. Continuity in Administrative Personnel, 1922-1934

	Total Civil Service	Transferred Civil Servants	
		No.	%
April 1, 1922	20,634	20,415	98.9
January 1, 1934	19,618	9,823	50.1

Sources: The table is based upon data contained in: Irish Free State, *Commission of Inquiry into the Civil Service, 1932-1935, Volume 1. Interim and Final Report: With Appendices;* Table (b). Third Appendix: 196. The total of transferred civil servants given for 1922 includes the staffs of the Land Commission and the Revenue Services, not technically transferred until April 1, 1923. These are also included in the total civil service, together with 131 persons who had served under Dail Eireann in the pre-Treaty period and 88 persons formerly in the British Civil Service who had left it on political grounds and returned to service between April 1, 1922, and October 1, 1923. The 1934 figure for the total civil service will be found on page 67 of the report. All totals exclude the so-called industrial classes of the civil service.

The extent of the inheritance is indicated by Table 3. As of January 1, 1934, two years after De Valera had taken office, 50.1 per cent of the civil service outside the industrial classes consisted of persons originally recruited under the British Government. Since the most important positions tended to be held by men with longer service, the proportion was considerably higher in the top ranks. Not surprisingly, De Valera complained that his party's advent to office was handicapped by unsympathetic administrative personnel[23] but he had promised there would be no political dismissals from the civil service and he respected that promise.

In only one way did De Valera disturb the existing civil service arrangements. In addition to recruitment by open competition and selection the Civil Service Regulation Acts provided an exceptional method of appointment by which the Executive Council, upon the recommendation of a minister, might declare it in the public interest that a particular person be appointed; the Commission would then issue a certificate of qualification without examination or selection. The limited use made of this procedure may be estimated from the report of the Commission of Inquiry into the Civil Service. "According to particulars furnished to us the power was exercised in 154 cases from 8th August 1923, up to the 31st December 1934. Of these cases 107 concerned persons who had formerly been in the Civil Service but had left it for political or similar reasons and were reinstated by exercise of this power. Of the other 47 cases the great majority were those of officers who had served for a considerable time as temporary Civil Servants, (Irish Free State, Commission of Inquiry into the Civil Service, 1932-1935: 110)."[24]

The very restricted impact of De Valera's election upon the civil service can be suggested in one other way. Retirements from the civil service were regulated by Article 10 of the Treaty. For some time early retirements were permitted "in consequence of the change of government".

The Free State objected, however, to the open-ended character of the opportunity for self-determined retirement. Following lengthy legal proceedings in both the Irish Free State Supreme Court and the British Privy Council the two governments came to an agreement "interpreting

TABLE 4. Retirements of Transferred Civil Servants under Article 10 of the Treaty

	In consequence of the change of government	Owing to worsened conditions of service	Total
1922	39	–	39
1923	689	2	691
1924	209	5	214
1925	43	–	43
1926	1	–	1
1927	6	1	7
1928	4	–	4
1929	4	–	4
1930	286	7	293
1931	–	2	2
1932	–	–	–
1933	–	43	43
1934	–	64	64

Source: Data are taken from Irish Free State, *Commission of Inquiry into the Civil Service, 1932-1935 Volume I, Interim and Final Reports: With Appendices:* Table (a), Third Appendix: 196.

and supplementing" Article 10. The new agreement limited the time for giving notice of intention to retire to December 5, 1929. Retirement was still permitted "owing to worsened conditions of service". Table 4 enumerates the number of retirements under each heading from 1922 through to 1934. Obviously De Valera's coming to office stimulated some retirements, but the number is quite small in relation to the near 10,000 transferred civil servants still in service at the time.

The effect of such continuity of administrative personnel could hardly be other than of a stabilizing and conservatizing character. The Irish Free State Commission of Inquiry into the Civil Service (1932-1935: 61) concluded:

> The passing of the State Service into the control of a native Government, however revolutionary it might have been as a step in the political development of the nation, entailed, broadly speaking, no immediate disturbance of any fundamental kind in the daily work of the average Civil Servant. Under changed master the same main tasks of administration continued to be performed by the same staffs on the same general lines of organization and procedure.

Not everyone was happy with this situation. One dissenter on the Commission, L. J. Duffy, quoted the same passage and added: "Unfortunately, that statement is true in detail and its implications are undeniable". Its immediate effect in 1932, however, was to smooth and ease the transition of government.[25]

If the acceptance of the change of government by the politicians is described as "surprising", and the behaviour of the civil service as "remarkable", some new adjective must be found to fit the army. In some ways the willingness of the army to accept the change was the most crucial — since it was here that the power to stage a *coup d'état* resided — and the most difficult to explain. The army had been created to fight the civil war. It had not been a pleasant war. Even today, more than fifty years later, a more or less dispassionate series of newspaper articles on the formation of the Free State Army will precipitate an acrimonious correspondence, beginning with: ". . . but who was responsible for the atrocities in Kerry?" (See Irwin, 1966.)[26] And the irony of the transfer of authority was heightened when De Valera designated as minister for defence the former commander-in-chief of the Republican forces, Frank Aiken. (In Aiken's case the irony was more apparent than real; he had been the last divisional commander to maintain neutrality in the civil war and assumed the position of IRA chief-of-staff only after the war was lost.) How then can the failure of the army to intervene be explained?

The first thing to be said is that the army did attempt to intervene, but the intervention came in 1924, not 1932. On Thursday, March 6, 1924 at 10 p.m. President Cosgrave was handed an ultimatum in his office at Government Buildings:

Sir — On behalf of the IRA Organization we have been instructed to present the following ultimatum to the Government of Saorstat Eireann:— Briefly our position is this:— The IRA only accepted the Treaty as a means of achieving its objects — namely, to secure and maintain a Republican form of Government in this country.
After many months of discussion with your Government it is our considered opinion that your Government has not these objects in view and that their policy is not reconcilable with the Irish people's acceptance of the Treaty.
Furthermore, our interpretation of the Treaty was that expressed by the late Commander-in-chief, General Michael Collins, when he stated "I have taken an oath of allegiance to the Irish Republic and that oath I will keep, Treaty or no Treaty". We claim Michael Collins as our leader and again remind you that even after the Treaty was signed that drastic action was taken against enemies of the unity and complete independence of our country. Both in oath and honour bound, it is our duty to continue his policy, and therefore present this ultimatum, to which we require a reply by 12 noon, 10th March, 1924.
We demand a conference with representatives of your Government to discuss our interpretation of the Treaty on the following

conditions:— (a) The removal of the Army Council; (b) The immediate suspension of army demobilization and reorganization.

In the event of your Government rejecting these proposals we will take such action that will make clear to the Irish people that we are not renegades or traitors to the ideals that induced them to accept the Treaty.

Our Organization fully realizes the seriousness of the action that we may be compelled to take, but we can no longer be party to the treachery that threatens to destroy the aspirations of the nation.

> Liam Tobin, Major-General
> President of the Executive Council
>
> C. F. Dalton, Col.,
> Secretary to the Executive Council
> (Irish Republican Army Organization,
> no date: 12).[27]

The story of the 1924 mutiny is a tangled one, and one that still cannot be completely straightened out. It requires some reference to the Irish Republican Brotherhood or IRB. The Brotherhood was a clandestine revolutionary movement. In conjunction with its Irish-American counterpart, Clan na Gael, it kept alive the Republican movement in Ireland from the 19th to the 20th century. The Easter Rising of 1916 in Dublin was largely the work of the IRB. After the Irish Volunteers (later popularly renamed the IRA) and the Sinn Fein political organization came together in 1917 in a public Republican movement De Valera and other leaders argued that a secret society was no longer needed and urged that the IRB be disbanded. Michael Collins disagreed and maintained an IRB network within the army. Much of Collins' influence derived from his leadership in the Brotherhood and it was one of the major forces responsible for the ratification of the Treaty. Significantly, the official resolution of the Supreme Council of the IRB, reiterating its support of the Treaty, explained it with the sentence: "It has always been the policy of the organization to make use of all instruments, political and otherwise, which are likely to aid in the attainment of its final end, i.e., 'A Free Independent Republican Government in Ireland' ". (Lynch, 1957; O'Donoghue 1954: 186-195).

Despite the pro-Treaty position of the Supreme Council the Brotherhood continued to provide one of the major links between Collins and the anti-Treaty forces. Even more remarkably it continued to function as such through the civil war. After Collins' death his place of leadership in the IRB was largely assumed by General Richard Mulcahy, the minister for defence. Mulcahy sought to follow Collins' policy of seeking agreement with the Republicans. On one occasion Tom Barry, a Republican military commander, communicated through Lt. General O Murthuile a proposal for the creation of a new "National Organization" in which the best elements of both sides could come together. Mulcahy found the plan attractive because, as he noted, the policy of the IRB "was fully controlled by us" and referred the plan to Cosgrave, O'Higgins, and Eoin MacNeill. They were unimpressed. At another point in the war Mulcahy met in conference with De Valera despite a Cabinet agreement not to hold meetings with individual Republican leaders. Nothing came of the meeting, but it generated tension within the Free State government. With his strength in the army, however, Mulcahy possessed an independent base of power.[28]

By this time the army consisted of two elements: first, those who, like Mulcahy, had fought in the struggle for national independence against Great Britain and had followed Collins into the Free State; second, those who had first been recruited as paid soldiers in the Free State Army. Many of the latter were Irish veterans of the British Army in France. The inevitable strains between the two groups were heightened at the end of the war when the Free State Army was to be reduced in size. The peak civil war strength of the army had been 55,000 troops and 3,300 officers. Demobilization called for a reduction to 18,000 troops and 1,300 officers. The process was to be completed on March 7 when 1,900 officers were scheduled to be discharged. Although priority in continued service had been given to those who had fought against Great Britain, not all who claimed national service were retained. Many reductions in rank were inevitable. And the Republican-minded officers objected to the political implications of the demobilization of the army. Collins had never accepted the partition of Ireland. Even after the Treaty he had continued to support military action in the North; co-operation in combined operations in Northern Ireland had been one of the factors delaying the outbreak of shooting between pro-Treaty and anti-Treaty elements in the army (O'Connor 1965: 157-158, 167, 171-172, 173-175, O'Donoghue, 1954: 247-254). Many army men were ready for "another round" with Great Britain, particularly if the alternative was peacetime unemployment.

The conflict within the army spilled over when Mulcahy and the Army Council began to extend the organization of the IRB within the army, but left out of their plans some of the veterans of the old IRA. Interestingly enough, the first reaction of the dissidents was to ask for representation within the Brotherhood (Irish Republican Army Organization, no date: 6). When that demand was not met to their satisfaction, they turned to the government, charging that the Army Council, dominated by IRB members, was discriminating against non-IRB members in dismissals and reductions in rank. The failure of the government to take action precipitated the mutiny. The cause of the mutineers was championed within the Cabinet by Joseph McGrath, the minister for industry and commerce. On the other side Mulcahy was, of course, himself a Cabinet member and the responsible minister.

The Cabinet replied to the ultimatum by ordering the arrest of Tobin and Dalton. Eoin O'Duffy was appointed General Officer Commanding the Defence Forces and Inspector General of the Forces. McGrath resigned from the Cabinet. Officers deserted their barracks with stolen arms at Gormanston, Clonmel, Baldonnel, and Roscommon. Just under a hundred officers resigned, including Major General McSweeney, the officer commanding Baldonnel aerodrome. With McGrath acting as intermediary a compromise solution was negotiated with the mutineers: the Cabinet promised an inquiry into the administration of the army and no victimization of the mutineers, and the mutiny was called off. A few days later troops under the command of the Army Council raided Devlin's, a public house in Parnell Street that was the headquarters of the self-styled "Old IRA" faction that had staged the mutiny. Since the raid was made without authority from O'Duffy the Cabinet dismissed the Army Council, consisting of the chief of staff, adjutant general, and quartermaster general. Mulcahy tendered his resignation. "Neutral" officers were appointed to the Army Council and the government, under changed circumstances, repudiated its agreement to restore the mutineers to service. Both the IRB and the "Old IRA" officers were removed from the positions of highest command.

Although it is difficult to evaluate the precise effect of the events of 1924 upon the position of the army eight years later it is obvious there is some relationship. The net effect was to remove from the army its most political elements. Their attitude toward the political process is suggested by an excerpt from a pamphlet later published by the "Old IRA" group: " 'Soldiers must not meddle in politics.' We have heard no such formulas from our soldier-patriot, Michael Collins, when we were fighting with him for Irish freedom against the British. Till the national ideals are satisfied we are patriots, not politicians" (Irish Republican Army Organization, no date: 16). In one sense, of course, in their devotion to the Republic, the "Old IRA" officers were closer to Fianna Fail than to Cumann na nGaedhal, but that is hardly a reason to believe their retention in the army would have eased the transition of 1932. They had already made their choice of sides in 1922, nor was De Valera any more prepared than Cosgrave to fight to end partition.

On the other hand, it would be a mistake to assume that an IRB Army Council would have resisted in 1932. With remarkable lack of guile the government in 1924 dismissed its Army Council without taking any precautions against a *coup d'état* from that source − and suffered no untoward consequences. When a member of the staff of the quartermaster general, Sean Muthuile, talked excitedly of refusing to accept such unjust treatment, he is alleged to have found himself rebuked by his chief. And General Mulcahy, who had returned to the Cabinet as minister for local government in 1927, was himself a member of the Cosgrave government which yielded power peacefully in 1932. Yet it is plain that 1924 carried onward a process that had begun with the civil war, the peeling away, layer by layer, of politically-minded volunteers from what was becoming increasingly a professional army. The process was continued through the late twenties as the army shifted from the excitement of war and civil war to the routine of peacetime training. Arrangements were made to send officers to U.S. military training schools for subsequent use as instructors in an Irish Military College and the education of officers was regularized. The position of the army was also sharply changed by its altered relationship with the British Army. From its original status as an Irish Republican Army engaged in a struggle for independence from Great Britain, the Free State Army was now more and more involved with the British Army in discussions of the mutual problems of imperial defence.

It is important to note, however, that the more professional character of the army did not mean that it was developing into a separate military class. Such a military class did exist in Ireland in an Anglo-Irish gentry that had provided officers to the British Army for generations. If the Free State Army had drawn heavily upon the services of that group or had developed a separate class base of a comparable kind, a quite different situation would have arisen in 1932. It did not, and the army remained highly democratic in recruitment. Returning to Ireland in the early 1930s after some years abroad Sean O'Faolain remarked on the changes he saw: "In the old days one saw the subalterns in the grandstand at the Curragh or Punchestown. Now one saw young fellows with the country blush of health on their cheeks, strolling among the crowds in and out among the roulette tables and the trick-o'-the-loop men. Not one of them had a private income. One sees a major-general riding in the trams − possibly with his youngster on his knee − a thing unknown, and indeed forbidden to the British Army," (O'Faolain, 1939: 163).

The change was an important one. Because the army was a cross-section of the general public, it shared the same political culture as the general public. That culture assumed the subordination of the military to the political. The army simply consisted of those who had happened to be separated out into an army career by the accidents of the time and circumstance. General Michael Brennan, the chief of staff in 1932 when the change of government took place, illustrates the point. At one time during the struggle for independence he occupied an anomalous dual position; he was simultaneously the Sinn Fein chairman of the Clare County Council and the commander of an IRA flying column. In the years after the Treaty he remained with the army. He became a military professional. But he did not abandon thereby the general political values of the society from which he had come.

This account of the change of government in Ireland in 1932 is incomplete in several ways. On its own terms it is incomplete; there are numerous unanswered questions still left before the peacefulness of the transition can be explained. It is also incomplete as an explanation of the establishment of stable democratic institutions in Ireland; before that process was complete it was necessary for De Valera to demonstrate that he could tolerate even an obstreperous opposition – in the thirties – and was as prepared to yield power – in 1948 – as to take it. Finally, it is incomplete in that no effort has been made to relate the Irish experience to the generalizations existent in the literature concerning the evolution of new nations.

The principal purpose of the paper is, however, to suggest the utility of the last-named possibility. Ireland is a new nation and has faced in the 20th century the same problems of institution-building that have confronted other nations of which more has been written. Although national pride has prevented Ireland's designation as economically underdeveloped, it is not a wealthy nation. At the same time it is a nation which is culturally tied to the West, not through the modernization of an elite, but through the pervasive involvement of the whole population in Western civilization. And it provides the limiting case for generalizations about political development: the poor new nation that has subordinated its army to its government, that has created a viable national administrative structure, and that has accepted the practice of party alternation in government.

Notes

1. It would be a mistake to assume the oversight results from Irish provincialism. American works on Ireland treat the subject in just the same way (see also Bromage, 1956). Most surprising is the omission of any reference to the significance of the change of government in Moss (1933) one of the first modern studies of political party organization and written at the time. In effect Moss treats the Irish party system simply as another established parliamentary democracy. The original dust jacket provides an interesting contrast: "Party dictatorships have swept Communist Russia, Fascist Italy, Nazi Germany ... and Ireland? Election after election the Soldiers of Destiny have marched to victory with De Valera. They sing, 'We will crown De Valera King of Ireland!' They charge their political opponents with treason

to Ireland's cause. He who is not De Valera's friend is Ireland's enemy! Here, in embryo, are all the elements of the 'party state' — the most significant political phenomenon of our time".

2. The text of the "Articles of Agreement for a Treaty between Great Britain and Ireland", plus the Free State Constitution, which was subsequently submitted to the British Government for approval, will be found in Kohn (1932). Although Document No. 2 was debated in secret and then withdrawn from publication its text is included as Appendix III of O'Hegarty (1924).

3. These figures are taken from Coogan (1966: 47, 51). The events of the Treaty negotiation, ratification, and consequences — the central fact of modern Irish political history — have been told and retold in many places, but nowhere else with the emotional intensity of O'Connor (1965). The most complete account of the Treaty negotiations will be found in Pakenham (1935) and the fullest record of the military operations in O'Donoghue (1954: 255-310).

4. Although several sources discuss the public political events of this period, only limited attention has been given to the developments within the Republican camp. The principal source is Moss (1933). The circumstances leading to the creation of Fianna Fail are described from De Valera's viewpoint in Bromage (1956: 208-244) and O'Faolain (1939: 111-129), and from the viewpoint of a Fianna Fail backbencher in Briscoe and Hatch (1959: 222-244).

5. The 1932 general election campaign is the subject of Chapter VI of Moss (1933: 173-88). The party statements to the electors by Cumann na nGaedhal, Fianna Fail, and Labour are reprinted in Moss (1933: 201-216).

6. In addition to the sources specifically cited in this section the author has relied upon interviews conducted in Dublin during the winter of 1965-1966 with Eamon De Valera, president of the executive council in the Fianna Fail government (then President of the Republic of Ireland); Frank Aiken, minister for defence in the De Valera government (then Tanaiste and minister for external affairs); Ernest Blythe, minister for finance, minister for posts and telegraphs, and vice-president of the executive council in the outgoing Cosgrave government; Gerald Boland, parliamentary secretary to the president of the executive council and to the minister for defence in the De Valera government; General Michael Brennan, chief of staff, National Army, 1932; John A. Costello, KC, attorney general to the Cosgrave government (subsequently An Taoiseach, 1948-1951, 1954-1957); Professor Michael Hayes, chairman of Dail Eireann, 1922-1932; Sean Lemass, minister for industry and commerce in the De Valera government (then An Taoiseach); Sean MacEntee, minister for finance in the De Valera government; General Richard Mulcahy, minister for local government and public health in the Cosgrave government; and Dr. James Ryan, minister for agriculture in the De Valera government.

7. Other sources confirm that the Archbishop of Dublin was asked by some Fianna Fail leaders to exercise his good offices for a peaceful change of government.

8. This section of the book was first published in 1944. MacManus died in 1951 and more recent editions of the book have been produced by the addition of chapters by David O'Neill concerning subsequent events. From the author's statement of appreciation to the librarian of *The Irish Press* it may be surmised that the charges of conspiracy made by MacManus reflect some of the same sources as the similar charge earlier made in that newspaper.

9. Since Mulcahy and Blythe were members of opposed factions within the government, the two stories would seem to be quite distinct.

10. MacManus (1962: 282-283) acknowledges as much. On the page following the charge of conspiracy, he writes:

> What sort of relations, people asked, were likely to develop between the Army and the new Minister for Defence? The Higher Command was composed almost entirely of men who had fought against the forces of which he had been Chief of Staff in the Civil War. Would these men give him the same loyalty that they had given his predecessor? These were natural questions, but they were soon answered. In his administration of Army affairs, big bluff Frank Aiken achieved a striking personal triumph within a remarkably short space of time. De Valera had made it clear on coming into office that he had no intention whatever of adopting a "spoils system", and even if in the Civil Service and the Army there were men in key positions who were his personal enemies, no official action would be taken against them so long as they served the State loyally. He believed, with Edmund Burke, that "magnanimity in politics is not seldom the truest wisdom". So the civil servants and the Army officers retained their posts and the governmental machine began to function smoothly. Frank Aiken became an immensely popular Minister for Defence and all danger of a military coup disappeared. From now onwards the Army was to be the Army of the state, not of a party.

11. In a review of Coogan's *Ireland Since the Rising* Ernest Blythe (1966a) noted that the reasons for O'Duffy's dismissal have never been satisfactorily explained, and added:

> Though there was great Opposition indignation at General O'Duffy's removal from office, it is not to be assumed that Fianna Fail dismissed him without reasonable cause. Originally a most excellent police officer, he had tended after the death of Kevin O'Higgins and after working for a less resolute Minister, to become difficult; and, on one occasion, it had to be made clear to him that the Cumann na nGael Government would, if necessary, find a way out of an impasse by appointing a new head of the Civic Guard.

O'Higgins's biographer notes that O'Higgins, who appointed O'Duffy to the post, also found him insubordinate at times and threatened to dismiss him (White, 1966: 231).

12. The other nations in the category are Australia, Belgium, Canada, Denmark, Luxembourg, the Netherlands, New Zealand, Norway, Sweden, Switzerland, the United Kingdom, and the United States. Unstable democracies and dictatorships are Albania, Austria, Bulgaria, Czechoslovakia, Finland, France, Germany, Greece, Hungary, Iceland, Italy, Poland, Portugal, Rumania, Spain, the USSR, and Yugoslavia. It is not altogether clear how Ireland qualifies as a stable democracy since Lipset (1963: 30 with footnote) explains:

> The main criteria used to define European democracies are the uninterrupted continuation of political democracy since World War I *and* the absence over the past twenty-five years of a major political movement opposed to the democratic "rules of the game" . . . The latter requirement means that no totalitarian movement, either fascist or communist, received 20% of the vote during this time. Actually all the European nations falling on the democratic side of the continuum had totalitarian movements which secured less than 7% of the vote.

Since, however, the sense of the classification is substantially identical with the interpretation advanced in this paper, the same two categories have been employed.

13. This was Cosgrave's statement made at the time of O'Higgins's assassination on the basis of secret reports from the police (Gwynn, 1928: 155-160).

14. O'Donnell (1963) is one of the few published accounts of these events.

15. With some justice Donal O'Sullivan (1940: 321) comments of the next (1933) general election that it "was the first general election in which class issues were raised". The reaction is reminiscent of the Republican response to Roosevelt.

16. Here Briscoe provides a graphic account of the effects of police harassment upon former members of the anti-Treaty forces.

17. In respect to the provisions for a commission to settle the boundary with Northern Ireland and concerning the Irish share of the British national debt.

18. As the political culture of modern Ireland is more clearly mapped, better evidence will become available. In the spring of 1966 students in the School of Public Administration, Dublin, conducted an opinion survey under my direction, interviewing 300 respondents drawn on a random basis from the electoral register of the municipal corporation of Dublin. The bulk of the questionnaire was concerned with political culture and made use of questions employed earlier in Almond and Verba (1963).

19. Major Bryan Cooper, who had been a Unionist member of Parliament prior to the establishment of the Free State, joined Cumann na nGaedhal in 1927 after first winning election as an independent but cannot be described as a leader in the government party.

20. The development of the Republican Dail and the subsequent disputes over legitimacy are discussed in McCracken (1958: 19-66).

21. Sean O'Faolain (1939: 167-168) has commented:

Another effect of the split has been that the Catholic Church gained tremendous influence in the new Ireland. It is the greatest organized body of power in the country, and inevitably the infant Free State, faced by a civil war, had to angle for its support. There was really very little need to angle. The Church in every country will always support, to the limit of human justice, established government. That is natural and proper. Had there been no split the Church would, in all probability, have had much less influence of a purely political nature ... One might, therefore, expect that on De Valera's rise to power the influence of the Church would decline. It has not done so. For one thing it was too firmly consolidated in power after ten years of the Free State. For another thing even De Valera in fighting his way back had to court it — one speaks only in terms of politics.

22. Chapter 1, "The Administrative Framework and the Civil Service", provides a general discussion of the situation at this time.

23. See the dissent by L. J. Duffy (Irish Free State, Commission of Inquiry into the Civil Service, 1932-1935: 205-206).

24. It should be pointed out that these figures greatly understate the number of positions made available to the De Valera government for appointment. The expansion of state services and in particular the creation of independent agencies, the so-called state-sponsored bodies, created many new government jobs.

25. One incidental effect of this continuity in administration should be noted. Since elections are administered in Ireland on the British rather than the American model, i.e., by professional government employees rather than by party amateurs, the civil service assumed responsibility for the counting of ballots throughout this period. Although some intimidation of candidates and, to a lesser extent, of voters occurred, particularly in the earlier elections, no serious question was raised in any election during this troubled period concerning the accuracy of the count.

26. This series with the letters it provoked is one of the few published sources of information concerning the Free State Army of this perod, but see also Chapter 12,

"The Irish Army," in Gwynn (1928: 176-190).

27. No full account of the Army Mutiny of 1924 yet exists; the most detailed published report is that found in White (1966: 122-123, 156-169), but is written entirely from one viewpoint, that of O'Higgins. Other sources include: Murdoch (1965); Blythe (1966b); "Black Raven" (1966); and Coogan (1966: 56-60). Bretherton (1925) is wild and most often inaccurate, but, as Thomas Johnson remarked at one time in the Dail, Bretherton sometimes "got hold of information".

28. Kevin O'Higgins (Dail Eireann, Parliamentary Debates: Official Report, 7: 3110) later declared: "I could not get away from the impression that the Minister for Defence came to the Executive Council, not so much as a colleague, to do business with colleagues, as in the capacity of a delegate – almost as a man coming to the Executive Council who held a watching brief for a particular organization, a watching brief for the Army in the Executive Council".

References

ALMOND, G. and S. VERBA (1963) The Civic Culture. Princeton: Princeton University Press.

"BLACK RAVEN" (1966) "Army Mutiny – 1924," *The Irish Times* (April 20).

BLYTHE, E. (1966a) "Anatomy of Ireland," *The Irish Times* (April 18).

BLYTHE, E. (1966b) "Mr. Joseph McGrath: An Appreciation," *The Irish Times* (March 28).

BRETHERTON, C. H. (1925) The Real Ireland. London: A. & C. Black Ltd.

BRISCOE, R. with A. HATCH (1959) For the Life of Me. London: Longmans, Green.

BROMAGE, M. C. (1956) De Valera and the March of a Nation. New York: Noonday Press.

COOGAN, T. P. (1966) Ireland Since the Rising. New York: Frederick A. Praeger.

DAHL, R. A. [ed.] (1966) Political Oppositions in Western Democracies. New Haven: Yale University Press.

DAIL EIREANN, Parliamentary Debates: Official Report.

GWYNN, D. (1928) The Irish Free State, 1922-1927. London: Macmillan.

GWYNN, D. (1933) De Valera. London: Jarrolds.

HOGAN, J. (1945) Election and Representation. Oxford: Cork University Press and B. J. Blackwell.

INGLIS, B. (1965) The Story of Ireland (2nd ed.). London: Faber & Faber.

IRISH FREE STATE. Commission of Inquiry into the Civil Service, 1932-1935. Interim and Final Reports: With Appendices. Volume I. Dublin: The Stationery Office.

IRISH REPUBLICAN ARMY ORGANIZATION (no date). The Truth about the Army Crisis (Official) with a Foreword by Major-General Liam Tobin. Dublin: 12.

IRWIN, S. P. (1966) "The Birth of an Army," *The Irish Times* (January 3 and 4; with correspondence January 4, 6, 7, 10, 13, 14, 15, 17, 18, 21, 24, 26, 27, 31 and February 1).

KOHN, L. (1932) The Constitution of the Irish Free State. London: George Allen & Unwin: 389-418.

LARKIN, E. (1965) James Larkin: Irish Labour Leader, 1876-1947. London: Routledge & Kegan Paul.

LIPSET, S. M. (1963) Political Man: The Social Bases of Politics. Garden City, New

York: Doubleday & Company: Anchor Books (first published, 1960).

LYNCH, D. (1957) (F. O'DONOGHUE, ed.) The IRB and the 1916 Insurrection. Cork: Mercier Press.

McCRAKEN, J. L. (1958) Representative Government in Ireland: A Study of Dail Eireann, 1919-1948. London: Oxford University Press.

McDOWELL, R. B. (1964) The Irish Administration, 1801-1914. London: Routledge & Kegan Paul.

MACMANUS, M. J. (1962) Eamon De Valera: A Biography (revised edition). Dublin: Talbot Press.

MOSS, W. (1933) Political Parties in the Irish Free State. New York: Columbia University Press.

MURDOCH, J. (1965) "Mutiny of the Generals" (series), *The Sunday Press*. Dublin (October 31; November 7, 14, 21, 28; December 5).

O'CONNOR, F. (1965) The Big Fellow: Michael Collins and the Irish Revolution (revised edition). Dublin: Clonmore & Reynolds.

O'DONNELL, P. (1963) There Will Be Another Day. Dublin: Dolmen Press.

O'DONOGHUE, F. (1954) No Other Law (The Story of Liam Lynch and the Irish Republican Army, 1916-1923). Dublin: Irish Press.

O'FAOLAIN, S. (1939) De Valera. Harmondsworth, London: Penguin Books.

O'HEGARTY, P. S. (1924) The Victory of Sinn Fein. Dublin: Talbot Press: 210-218.

O'SULLIVAN, D. (1940) The Irish Free State and Its Senate: A Study in Contemporary Politics. London: Faber & Faber: 285.

PAKENHAM, F. (1935) Peace By Ordeal. London: Jonathan Cape.

RUSSETT, B. M., H. ALKER JR., K. W. DEUTSCH, and H. D. LASSWELL (1964) World Handbook of Political and Social Indicators. New Haven: Yale University Press.

THE ROUND TABLE: A Quarterly Review of the Politics of the British Commonwealth (1931-1932) "Ireland and the Treaty: I. The Result of the Election". Volume 22; and "The Irish Free State: I. The General Election," Volume 22.

WHITE, T. DE V. (1966) Kevin O'Higgins. Tralee: Anvil Books.

Frank Munger is Professor of Political Science at the University of
North Carolina, Chapel Hill.